MW01171863

Native Spiritual Realms: A Guide to Native American Paranormal

by Durinda Stewart

ISBN 979-8-88940-905-2

9 798889 409052

Table of Contents

Dedication

To my husband, Joe, for being my Rock through it all.

Also, to my ancestors, who taught me love of all in nature.

Reviews

"It is an enjoyable journey with the author as she connects with her heritage and investigates the legends and supernatural experiences of the Native Americans. She portrays the wisdom of the Native American peoples, in their approach to the paranormal with respect and understanding, an example for all to follow."

-Joseph Stewart
Author of *Demons: A Secular Look* (authorjosephstewart.com)
Founder of *Society of Demonologists* (societyofdemonologists.org)

"Understanding our DNA is tantamount to understanding our roots in the land. The voices of our predecessors resonate in both our genetic makeup and the earth they once trod upon. This connection is a powerful presence for those of us attuned to it, allowing us to unravel the secrets they encountered and draw parallels to our modern world. Durinda skillfully captures this concept in her writing, bridging the gap between past and present and sharing these ancestral voices with a broader audience."

-Barry Fitzgerald,
Author, Director, Editor, and Researcher
The Deceptions of Gods and Men

"This is an incredibly insightful book not only useful as a resource tool but also bringing a better understanding of Native American history and how they perceived the world around them, which clearly demonstrates that they believed they shared this reality with numerous other spiritual and supernatural forces; some of which even identifies the UFO phenomenon. Has humanity throughout its years developed an ignorance to other conscious intelligence's around us and have we aloud ourselves to become limited in our perception of them? It would seem that in modern times we still may have these intelligence's around us but have given them little to no recognition, but on occasion some continue to experience them, possible giving them new names and terminologies. Such phenomena are still present and witnesses to their presence would rather attempt to ignore rather than incorporate them into our understanding of the world around us. I assure you, these phenomena never left, and we can learn so much from our ancient ancestors that seemingly had a far superior understanding of how we can coexist....

Durinda has provided detailed accounts of some of the most perplexing phenomena through the eyes of our Native American ancestors which can clearly still be identified today.
A well written, fascinating source of information. I thoroughly enjoyed it."

-Steve Mera
International TV & Radio Host, Actor, Freelance Journalist, International Lecturer & Head Tutor of the UFO Investigators Training Course (UITC)
Steve Mera's Official Website: http://www.stevemera.com

"I loved this book. So much information and insight packed into one small space. The author expertly weaves her own spiritual and paranormal experiences into the broader perspective of Native American spiritual belief and practice, making this an absolutely fascinating read."
-Melinda Simon

Forward

I met Durinda Stewart ten years ago at a mutual friend's *Wish Game* party, a metaphysical board game designed to pull from your subconscious any resistance to the wishes/dreams/goals you have in life, therefore making it easier for the Universe to connect you to your heart's desires. We immediately became good friends. From the start I was blown away by her extensive knowledge of all things supernatural, psychic, and alternative, so when she approached me to build her website and podcast, I was excited. Then she told me she was writing a book ... this book ... the one you are reading right now.

Not only is this book well written by an author who is an expert in the field of *Native Spiritual Paranormal*, but it is an important work, drawing on a rich history and critical narration of our world. Like me, humanity is drawn to the mysterious, the inexplicable, and the supernatural as it travels through the great expanse of existence. Tales of the paranormal have permeated our collective consciousness throughout history, acting as mirrors to reflect the depths of our hopes, fears, and beliefs.

There is a complex tapestry of myths, folklore, and experiences that cut over time and geography in the paranormal domain. However, inside this complex web, there exists a collection of stories that are particularly meaningful - the stories of Native Americans.

In "Native Spiritual Realms: A Guide to Native American Paranormal," Durinda extends an invitation for us to travel into the core of indigenous spirituality and wisdom. Stewart offers an engrossing examination of the paranormal beliefs and experiences among indigenous tribes, drawing on her substantial knowledge and profound respect for Native American culture.

In addition to being a compilation of paranormal events, this book is a monument to the tenacity, resourcefulness, and close ties to the natural world that characterize Native American spirituality. We are given a look into a world where the lines between the material and spiritual realms are blurred, where ancestors' whispers reverberate through the ages, and where the ground itself is charged with sacred energy thanks to Stewart's painstaking curation of stories, rituals, and customs.

More than just a book, "Native Spiritual Realms" is a bridge connecting two worlds that invites us to stop, pay attention, and respect the knowledge of our forebears, regardless of our race or creed. These chapters serve as a reminder of our interdependence with all living things as we come across the spirits of the ground, the keepers of the forests, and the defenders of old wisdom.

Let us approach this journey of discovery with humble hearts and open minds, prepared to absorb the knowledge of indigenous peoples and embrace the mysteries that exist beyond the realm of our comprehension.

I hope that reading "Native Spiritual Realms" will create a stirring, a pondering, and inspire appreciation for the intricate details of Native American culture and the deep insights it provides into the world of the paranormal.

Angela Malloy
(A Fellow Traveler)

Introduction

Have you ever wondered what lies beyond the veil of our reality? Those unexplained phenomena and whispered legends that have fascinated and bewildered us for centuries? Join me, Durinda Stewart, as we embark on a captivating journey into the realm of Native American paranormal.

As a native American psychic, ghost hunter, bigfoot enthusiast, and UFO aficionado, I have dedicated my life to unraveling the mysteries that dance in the shadows. I have traversed the ancient lands, mingled with spirits, and listened to the whispers of the wind. And now, I invite you to accompany me on a quest to understand the myths and stories that have shaped the native American paranormal.

In the depths of our existence, there exists a rich tapestry of legends and beliefs that have been passed down through the generations. These sacred tales tell of spirits that walk among us, unseen and yet deeply felt. They reveal a deep connection between the physical and spiritual realms, where dimensions intertwine and possibilities are boundless.

Native American cultures have long recognized the existence of a parallel existence – a world of spirits, creatures, and forces that coexist with our own. It is a delicate balance, teetering on the edge of spiritual harmony and chaos, where ancient wisdom and supernatural encounters collide in a breathtaking dance.

As we delve into the chapters of "Native Paranormal," we will encounter a multitude of beings – some benevolent, others mischievous, and a few that inspire terror in the hearts of those who dare to cross their paths. From the elusive Sasquatch, known as Bigfoot to many, to the enigmatic Skinwalkers, shapeshifters with malicious intent, the native American paranormal is a cornucopia of wonder and awe.

But it's not all fright and goosebumps. The native American paranormal also harbors a world of magic and guidance. Native American shamans, healers, and seers have long tapped into unseen energies to divine knowledge, protect their communities, and restore balance in times of strife. The stories recounted in this book will not only ignite your imagination but also provide insights into the interconnectedness of humanity, nature, and the spirit world.

Prepare yourself for a captivating exploration of haunted burial grounds, sacred caves, and forgotten ruins, where shadows flit and whispers beckon. Feel the thrill of encountering beings that defy the limitations of our mortal realm and glimpse into a universe that simultaneously frightens and mesmerizes.

With each page turned, you will find yourself drawn deeper into the mystique of the native American paranormal. You will witness the eerie glow of will-o'-the-wisps dancing on moonlit nights, hear the haunting melodies of supernatural flutes, and experience the chill of unseen hands brushing against your skin. But fear not, dear reader, for I shall be your guide, leading you safely through these ethereal realms and out into the dawn of understanding.

As we wander through these enchanted stories, let us not forget the profound respect with which these tales must be treated. They are not mere entertainment but a glimpse into the soul of a culture, a tribute to centuries of tradition and wisdom passed from one generation to the next. It is a privilege to walk alongside these storytellers, to honor the spirits that inhabit their words, and preserve the magic of their heritage.

So, my fellow seekers of the unknown, are you ready to embark on this extraordinary voyage into the native American paranormal? Together, let us delve into the depths of myths and stories that defy explanation and embrace the captivating enigma that lies within. Open your hearts and minds, for the journey begins here.

CHAPTER 1

Realm of Native American Paranormal

The Sacred Connection

I have always been aware of the deep spiritual bond that exists between my Native American heritage and the paranormal world. Not growing up on a reservation, because I was half white and half native. I had a spiritual mother and father, as well as grandparents from the reservation who adopted me as their own because of my native blood. My native father abandoned my white mother before I was born, but fortunately they immersed me in a culture that embraced and respected the supernatural. I learned that our connection to the spirit realm was not something to be feared or dismissed; rather, it was seen as an integral part of life, guiding and influencing our every step.

For centuries, Native American tribes across the continents have had a profound understanding and acceptance of the paranormal. Our ancestors knew that the natural world and the spiritual world were inseparable, interconnected in ways that modern society often fails to grasp. We believe that everything in the universe - from animals and plants to natural phenomena and celestial bodies - possesses a spirit or energy capable of communicating with us.

This belief in the sacred connection between humans and the paranormal and manifests in many facets of Native American culture. Rituals, ceremonies, and even everyday practices are deeply rooted in this connection. From the sacred dances performed to honor the spirits, to the use of visionary plants to facilitate communication with other realms, each activity is designed to maintain harmony and balance between our physical and spiritual existence.

One aspect of this connection that has captivated me for as long as I can remember is the ability to communicate with the spirits of our ancestors. As a native American psychic, I have honed my abilities to connect with the past and channel the wisdom and guidance of those who came before me. Through dreams, visions, and rituals, I have experienced the profound influence of our ancestors lingering on the ethereal plane, eager to guide and protect us.

My journey as a ghost hunter started as a way to honor this sacred connection. I believe that spirits are not to be feared or exorcised, but rather understood and respected. By investigating haunted places and communicating with the spirits that reside there, I seek to bridge the gap between the living and the dead, offering them peace and reassurance. In these investigations, I not only delve into the mysteries of the paranormal but also pay homage to my heritage and the knowledge passed down through generations.

My pursuits as a bigfoot and UFO hunter may seem unrelated to my Native American roots at first glance, but they too are connected to the sacred bond between our people and the supernatural. In indigenous legends, bigfoot and other cryptids are often referred to as guardians of the land, protectors of nature, and messengers from the spirit world. They are seen as physical manifestations of the spirits that watch over us, reminding us to respect and preserve the natural world.

Similarly, Native American traditions are rich with stories of celestial beings visiting the earth in the form of UFOs. These encounters are not viewed as aberrant or fictional but rather as spiritual experiences and reminders of the vastness of the universe and our place within it. Exploring the accounts of UFO sightings and encounters allows me to delve deeper into the concept of an interconnected cosmic existence and the existence of beings beyond our comprehension.

In Native American culture, the sacred connection to the paranormal is not restricted to a few chosen individuals but is accessible to all who seek it. It is a wellspring of knowledge and wisdom that has guided our people for millennia. Through my experiences as a Native American psychic, ghost hunter, bigfoot hunter, and UFO enthusiast, I strive to share this intricate web of connections with the world, hoping to inspire a deeper understanding and respect for the rich tapestry of the paranormal that intertwines with our lives.

The Power of Ancestors

When I visited the reservation, I often heard stories about our ancestors and their supernatural abilities. These tales fascinated and intrigued me, fueling my curiosity to delve deeper into the rich tapestry of native paranormal lore. In my quest for knowledge, I sought out the wisdom of tribal elders and shamans, eager to uncover the secrets hidden within our heritage.

Through my research and experiences, I have come to understand that the power of ancestors transcends time and space. They exist in a realm beyond our physical world, yet they have the ability to influence and guide us in profound ways. It is through their ancient wisdom that we are able to unveil hidden truths and gain a deeper understanding of the mysteries that surround us.

One of the most enlightening aspects of my journey has been connecting with the spirits of my own ancestors. Through meditation and ritual, I have been able to establish a dialogue with them and tap into the profound insights they offer. They have shared visions of long-forgotten rituals, rituals brimming with power and significance. They have shared sacred herbal remedies and healing practices that have been passed down through generations. It is as if they have become my spiritual mentors, guiding me towards a path of enlightenment and truth.

The wisdom and guidance that our ancestors offer is not limited to our own bloodline. They represent a collective consciousness of our entire Native American heritage, a source of knowledge that stretches back through the ages. By embracing their power and acknowledging their presence, we have the opportunity to tap into an unlimited reservoir of ancient wisdom.

Unveiling the ancient wisdom and guidance passed down through generations requires an open heart and mind. It necessitates stepping outside the confines of our mundane reality and embracing the supernatural. It is through this genuine connection with the spirit world that we can access the hidden truths, the profound insights that have been waiting to be revealed.

In my own journey, I have witnessed the transformative power of ancestral guidance. It has allowed me to gain a deeper understanding of my purpose on this earth, and to navigate the paranormal realms with confidence and clarity. I have encountered spirits that have revealed themselves during my ghost hunts. I have come face to face with the elusive bigfoot, feeling a deep sense of connection to this mythical being. And I have witnessed unexplainable UFO sightings, feeling the presence of ancient extraterrestrial beings who have been observing our planet for centuries.

The power of ancestors is not just a mystic concept; it is a tangible force that shapes our lives and influences our every decision. By embracing their presence and honoring their wisdom, we can tap into a wellspring of knowledge that will guide us towards a deeper understanding of ourselves and the world around us.

The Shaman's Journey

It all began when I received a cryptic message on an old parchment, seemingly woven from the fabric of time itself. The message was simple yet enigmatic, inviting me to partake in a spiritual expedition with the revered shamans of Native American tribes. Intrigued and filled with a sense of anticipation, I answered the call without any hesitation.

The journey took me deep into the heart of the wilderness, where the shamans, dressed in ritualistic attire adorned with feathers and beads, awaited my arrival. Surrounded by the sights and sounds of nature, we gathered around a sacred fire, its flames dancing and flickering in harmony with our collective spirits.

The shamans began by purifying the space, using aromatic herbs and sacred chants to cleanse our spirits and open the channels of communication with the spiritual realm. In this heightened state of awareness, we embarked on a journey of the mind, transcending the boundaries of time and space.

As the drumbeats reverberated through the night air, the shamans guided us through a series of ancient practices and rituals. They taught us to connect with the unseen forces that permeate the universe, to tap into the collective consciousness and harness the power of our intuition.

One of the most profound experiences during the Shaman's Journey was the visionary ceremony. Led by the shamans, we consumed a potent concoction of sacred plants, allowing us to transcend the limitations of the physical realm and explore the depths of our own consciousness. In this altered state, our senses heightened, and the veil between the seen and unseen worlds became thin.

During these ethereal travels, the shamans served as our guides, leading us through realms known only to them. They shared their sacred knowledge, ancient myths, and legends, intertwining their words with the very fabric of the cosmos. Their wisdom echoed through the chambers of my soul, stirring memories long forgotten and awakening a deep sense of connection to the spiritual heritage of my ancestors.

Through these spiritual encounters, I witnessed firsthand the intertwined relationship between humans and the supernatural. I learned that the spirits of the land are not mere tales passed down through generations but living, breathing entities that shape our reality in ways we could never fully comprehend.

The Shaman's Journey was not just a physical expedition; it was a pilgrimage of the soul. It was an opportunity to immerse myself in the ancient traditions and wisdom of the Native American tribes, to connect with the spirits of the land and honor the legacy of my ancestors.

As I emerged from the depths of this mystical adventure, I carried with me a newfound sense of purpose and an unshakeable belief in the power of the paranormal. The Shaman's Journey had left an indelible mark on my psyche, forever altering my perception of the supernatural. It was a reminder that our world is far more complex and intertwined with the unseen than we dare to imagine. And so, armed with this knowledge and my unwavering determination, I continued my quest as a Native American psychic, ghost hunter, Bigfoot seeker, and UFO enthusiast, exploring the mysteries that lay beyond the veil of the ordinary.

Spirit Animals

My journey into the realm of spirit animals started with research. I devoured countless books, delving deep into the annals of Native American history and spirituality. I learned that in their culture, animals were seen as sacred beings, messengers from the spirit world with their own unique qualities and traits. They were believed to possess great wisdom and power, capable of guiding and assisting humans on their paths.

According to Native American beliefs, each person is connected to a specific animal spirit, also known as a totem or power animal. This animal serves as a guide, a protector, and a source of spiritual strength. It is believed that these animals choose us, and through their presence in our lives, they offer us insight, support, and direction.

The more I delved into my research, the more I began to understand the intricate relationships between humans and animals in Native American culture. I learned that it wasn't just the physical attributes of an animal that determined its spiritual significance, but also the symbolism associated with it. For example, the bear was revered for its strength, courage, and protective nature, making it an ideal spirit animal for warriors. The eagle, representing freedom, vision, and wisdom, was associated with spiritual leaders and healers.

As I immersed myself in the teachings of Native American spirituality, I also sought knowledge from the elders within my community. I listened to their stories, their experiences, and their deep wisdom. They spoke of encounters with animal spirits, the messages they received, and the profound impact those encounters had on their lives. Their stories resonated deeply within me, reinforcing my own belief in the power of spirit animals.

But it wasn't enough for me to simply learn about spirit animals through books and stories. I had to experience their presence firsthand. I began spending time in nature, meditating, and connecting with the spirits that dwelled in the wilderness. This communion was a sacred process, a way for me to deepen my understanding and connection to the spiritual realm.

I vividly remember the first time I encountered my own spirit animal. It was during a solitary journey through a dense forest. As I walked in quiet contemplation, a majestic wolf emerged from the trees, its piercing eyes locked with mine. In that moment, I felt a surge of energy, a connection that transcended the physical realm. I knew then and there that the wolf would be my guide, my protector, and my spiritual companion. Wolves bring messages to me as well. For example, my stepfather was ill, and I had to drive around two hours to get to where he was staying in Michigan. Here, we have emergency drives for authorized vehicles on most highways, sometimes noted by stretches of highway where there are patches of trees between the right and left lane. On my journey to my stepfather's bedside, standing on that emergency drive, was a wolf watching me as I drove by. At the time, I wondered what he was trying to say to me. I thought it was a fluke until I came back that way several hours later and on the opposite side of the road was a wolf. My stepfather died the next day.

Since that profound encounter, my relationship with my spirit animal has continued to grow and evolve. The wolf has guided me through challenging times, offering me strength and courage when I needed it most. Its presence has become a constant source of inspiration and reassurance in my journey as a psychic, ghost hunter, Bigfoot hunter, and UFO enthusiast.

Through my research, experiences, and connections with elders, I have come to understand the immense significance of spirit animals in Native American culture. They are not just symbols or metaphors; they are living beings with their own unique spiritual essence. They hold the key to unlocking our own spiritual potential, guiding us towards our true purpose and helping us navigate the complexities of life.

In the pages that follow, I will continue to explore the world of spirit animals, diving deeper into their symbolism, their messages, and the profound impact they can have on our lives. Together, we will embark on a journey of spiritual discovery and uncover the mystical thread that connects us all to the vast web of existence.

The Veil Between Worlds

As a ghost hunter, I have spent countless nights exploring haunted locations, seeking evidence of entities that linger in the realm of the dead. Armed with my trusted EVP recorder, I navigate through dimly lit corridors and desolate rooms, listening intently for any voice from the other side. The air is thick with anticipation as I carefully document each flicker, each whisper, all in an effort to capture undeniable proof of the afterlife.

But my curiosity knows no bounds. My journey veers beyond the realm of ghosts and spirits. As a bigfoot hunter, I venture deep into the dense forests, following ancient tribal legends and relying on my innate intuition. I spend hours studying footprints, analyzing hair samples, and seeking out eyewitness testimonies. These creatures, elusive and mysterious, that have long fascinated me, believed by many to be guardians of a hidden realm, living on the fringe between our world and the supernatural. I am determined to uncover the truth that lies in the shadows of the towering trees.

My pursuit of the unknown does not stop there. UFOs, or unidentified flying objects, have intrigued and perplexed people for centuries. These ethereal crafts, said to be piloted by extraterrestrial beings, defy the laws of our physical world. As a researcher, I am relentless in studying eyewitness accounts, analyzing photographs and videos, and consulting with experts in the field. Each sighting brings me one step closer to understanding the enigma of these visitors from beyond our planet, and the profound impact they may have on the delicate balance between worlds.

The thin line that separates our physical realm from the spiritual is both captivating and treacherous. It is a boundary that I have dedicated my life to crossing, armed with knowledge passed down through generations, and honed through my own intrepid experiences. I have witnessed the magic and terror that exists on the other side of this veil, and I am driven to unveil the secrets it holds.

Through my investigations as a native paranormal expert, I have come to understand that the veil between worlds is not merely a physical barrier but also a metaphysical construct. It is a boundary created by the energy flow of the universe, and to cross it requires a delicate harmony of mind, body, and spirit. The ability to navigate this thin line is a gift bestowed upon those who possess a deep connection to the spiritual realm, a connection that transcends the limitations of our mortal existence.

As I continue my exploration into the realms beyond, I am thoughtful of the profound respect which must be held for the unknown. It is not just about uncovering the mysteries that lie in the shadows; it is about recognizing the interconnectedness of all beings, physical or otherwise. It is about acknowledging the delicate balance between worlds and treading lightly, with reverence and awe.

The thin line between the physical and spiritual realms beckons me forward, calling me to delve deeper into the mysteries that lie beyond. With each investigation, I am reminded of the power and potential that exists in the unseen. And as I navigate this ethereal terrain, I am guided by the knowledge that the answers I seek are not just about the physical evidence I uncover, but about the transformational journey that occurs within myself as I traverse the veil between worlds.

CHAPTER 2

Legendary Creature

Skinwalkers: Shape-Shifting Entities

My journey into the supernatural began with my Native American heritage, intertwining my spiritual connection with my relentless curiosity. As an enthusiast of everything occult related, I sought to uncover the hidden truths that lay beyond the veil of our earthly existence. The existence of skin-walkers, or Yee Naaldlooshii as they are known in the Navajo tongue, became the next chapter in my exploration of the unknown.

With an insatiable hunger for knowledge and a thirst for adventure, I embarked on a path of research, seeking out individuals who had encountered these shape-shifting entities firsthand. The first story that caught my attention was that of Annie Whitehorse, a young Navajo woman who had witnessed a skin-walker's terrifying transformation.

Annie's tale echoed through the barren deserts and tree-lined canyons of the reservation, leaving a trail of fear in its wake. She had been returning home late one night, her footsteps echoing in the eerie silence, when she caught a glimpse of movement out of the corner of her eye. Turning her gaze towards the darkness, she saw a figure emerge from the shadows. It was a creature like none she had ever seen before – half-human, half-animal, its eyes burning with an otherworldly intensity.

As the creature drew nearer, it morphed before Annie's eyes, its body contorting into an unnatural form. The sound of cracking bones filled the air as the skin-walker shed its human facade and transformed into a monstrous beast. Annie's heart raced as she watched the creature – now resembling a twisted hybrid of man and wolf – approach her with malevolent intent.

The encounter haunted Annie, leaving her restless and tormented by the memory of that fateful night. I sat with her, listening intently as she recounted every detail, her voice filled with a mixture of terror and awe. The profound effect the experience had on her was palpable; her words were infused with a deep-seated primal fear that could not be dismissed as mere superstition.

Drawing upon my psychic abilities, I sought to understand the supernatural abilities of skin-walkers and unravel the mysteries that shrouded them. This led me to uncover ancient legends and rituals, embedded in Navajo culture, which spoke of individuals who possessed the power to shape-shift into animals. These individuals were said to have bargained their souls with dark forces, gaining the ability to traverse the boundaries of the physical world.

The skin-walkers were believed to be malevolent souls, harnessing their shape-shifting abilities for wicked purposes. Legends warned of their insatiable hunger for power; their bloodlust and penchant for violence knew no bounds. They were said to be able to take on the form of any creature, whether it be a wolf, coyote, or even a bird, allowing them to move undetected through the vast desert landscape.

The acquisition of such knowledge only deepened my fascination with these shape-shifting entities. Each chilling tale I encountered brought me closer to understanding the intricacies of their supernatural abilities. I immersed myself in texts, delving into ancient folklore and consulting with fellow experts in the paranormal field, as I sought to piece together the puzzle of the skin-walkers.

As I continued my research, I realized that the skin-walkers were not merely creatures of myth and legend, but a tangible presence that lingered in the shadows, waiting for an opportunity to strike. They were far more than just stories whispered around campfires; they were a part of our reality, a dark and sinister chapter in the annals of Native American folklore.

Driven by a desire to protect my people and shed light on the hidden truths that lay dormant, I vowed to face these shape-shifting entities head on. The stories of their supernatural abilities would no longer be confined to whispered rumors; they would be unraveled and exposed for the world to see. I firmly believed that by understanding their powers, I would be better equipped to combat them and bring an end to the reign of terror they inflicted upon the reservation.

With each passing day, my resolve grew stronger. The chilling tales of skin-walkers and their supernatural abilities had become intertwined with my very soul, fueling my determination to expose their secrets. As I prepared to venture deeper into their realm, I knew that I was on the brink of a discovery that would forever change the way we perceive the paranormal.

Thunderbirds: Majestic Winged Guardians

As a native American I have always been drawn to the fascinating and mysterious world of the paranormal. Among the various legends that have captured my attention, the stories of the thunderbirds have always held a special place in my heart. These majestic, winged creatures, often described as enormous birds with wingspans that blot out the sun, have played a significant role in Native American mythology across different tribes.

The thunderbirds, also known as "Wakinyan," in Lakota or "Paloma" in the Abenaki tribe, have been revered as powerful and awe-inspiring guardians. According to ancient Native American legends, these magnificent beings reside in the sky, soaring through the clouds with their thunderous wings creating the rumble we associate with a thunderstorm. The menacing crack of lightning is believed to be the thunderbird's way of announcing its presence to the world.

Unveiling the legends surrounding the thunderbirds has been no easy feat. My research has taken me deep into the heart of Native American lore, delving into the stories passed down from generation to generation. What I discovered was a rich tapestry of tales that portrayed the thunderbirds not as mere creatures of myth, but as celestial beings with the power to shape the world.

One particular legend that struck me was the story of a young warrior from the Ojibwe tribe named Wiindigoog. As the tale goes, Wiindigoog's village was constantly plagued by attacks from rival tribes. The desperate villagers turned to the thunderbirds for protection, offering prayers and sacrifices to gain their favor. In response, the thunderbirds granted Wiindigoog a mystical feather, allowing him to call upon their strength and guidance whenever he needed it. With this newfound power, Wiindigoog became a fearless warrior, leading his tribe to victory against their adversaries.

Another legend hailed from the Hopi tribe, who believed that the thunderbirds were responsible for bringing rain and fertility to the land. They saw these majestic creatures as the protectors of their crops and the bringers of life-giving water. It was believed that during times of drought, the thunderbirds would send lightning bolts to split open the clouds, unleashing a torrential downpour that would rejuvenate the parched earth.

Throughout my journey of unraveling the mysteries surrounding thunderbirds, I have come across countless stories that highlight their role as guardians and protectors. From the Lakota Sioux who revered them as the winged guardians of the celestial realms, to the Navajo who saw them as the harbingers of good fortune, these powerful creatures have left an indelible mark on Native American traditions.

But the question remains: are thunderbirds simply mythological beings, or do they truly exist in the physical realm? As a dedicated paranormal investigator, I have spent countless nights searching for evidence of their presence. Footprints resembling giant bird claws, eyewitness accounts of seeing enormous bird-like creatures overhead, and even ancient petroglyphs depicting these majestic creatures have fueled my belief that there is more to this legend than meets the eye.

In the next chapter, we will delve deeper into the realm of physical evidence and eyewitness accounts, exploring the possibilities of encountering thunderbirds in the modern world. Join me as we continue to unravel the enigmatic legends of these majestic, winged guardians and shed light on the truth that lies behind the veil of Native American mythology.

Water Spirits: Guardians of Rivers and Lakes

My research into water spirits has been both extensive and eye-opening. Through ancient myths, legends, and personal experiences, I have come to understand the integral role these ethereal beings play in Native American spiritual beliefs. In many indigenous cultures, water spirits are considered to be guardians and protectors of the natural world, ensuring the balance and harmony of our planet.

One particular tribe that heavily honors water spirits is the Ojibwe. According to their mythology, there are numerous water spirits inhabiting the lakes and rivers of their ancestral lands. These spirits are believed to possess great powers and are revered by the Ojibwe people as sacred beings. While some water spirits are known to be benevolent and friendly, others are deemed more mischievous, often testing the mettle and wisdom of those who cross their paths.

The Ojibwe belief in the guardianship of water spirits is deeply ingrained in their tribal practices and rituals. They maintain a strong spiritual connection with the waters, offering prayers and offerings to these ancient beings in exchange for their protection and goodwill. It is believed that by appeasing the water spirits, a harmonious relationship can be maintained between the physical and spiritual realms.

In my own personal experiences, I have encountered the presence of water spirits on multiple occasions. One particularly memorable encounter took place during a late-night investigation at a secluded lake deep within the forested terrain. As I stood on the shoreline, I felt an overwhelming sense of calm wash over me, as if the very essence of the water itself was imbued with a serene energy. It was as if the spirits were whispering their ancient wisdom, sharing their secrets and insights with me.

Another intriguing aspect of water spirits is their role as healers. According to indigenous beliefs, water spirits possess the ability to purify both the physical and spiritual body. It is not uncommon for individuals to seek the spiritual guidance of these benevolent beings to cleanse their souls and restore their inner balance. Water is seen as a powerful conduit for healing, and the spirits that inhabit these watery realms are revered for their ability to bring solace and renewal to those in need.

In conclusion, delving into the depths of native American water spirits and their significance in spiritual beliefs has been a journey of profound discovery for me. The stories, myths, and experiences I have encountered have illuminated the vital role these ethereal beings play in our connection to nature and the supernatural realm. As I continue my quest as a native paranormal investigator, I am certain that further exploration into the realm of water spirits will continue to unveil awe-inspiring revelations and deepen my understanding of the intricate tapestry of native American spirituality.

Tricksters: Mischievous Spirits

My heart raced with anticipation as I delved deeper into the fascinating world of Native American folklore. The legends and stories passed down from generation to generation had always enchanted me, but it was the mischievous tricksters that intrigued me the most. These cunning spirits, known for their playful nature and clever tactics, had become a central focus of my research.

I had encountered my fair share of supernatural entities. However, the mischievous tricksters were unlike anything I had ever encountered before. Their powers transcended the physical realm, making them elusive and unpredictable. It was this enigmatic nature that piqued my curiosity and fueled my determination to unravel their secrets.

In my quest to uncover the truth, I immersed myself in countless ancient texts, oral traditions, and interviews with Native American elders. The more I learned, the clearer it became that the tricksters were not to be taken lightly. They were masters of illusion and deception, capable of manipulating both humans and spirits alike.

One tale that resonated deeply with me was the legend of the Coyote, a trickster known across various Native American tribes. The Coyote was a shapeshifter, assuming different forms and playing tricks on those he encountered. Some stories depicted him as a helpful guide, imparting wisdom, and valuable life lessons. Others portrayed him as cunning and conniving, leading unsuspecting victims astray for his own amusement.

Another disruptor that fascinated me was the Raven, revered in many Native American cultures for his mischievous acts. With his dark feathers glistening in the moonlight, he was both feared and respected. The Raven had an insatiable curiosity, always seeking to disrupt the natural order of things. His antics often resulted in chaos but occasionally brought forth transformation and rebirth.

Beyond the familiar figures of Coyote and Raven, I uncovered a whole host of lesser-known tricksters. There was the mischievous Hare, known for his quick wit and cleverness, often outsmarting those who crossed his path. The Spider Woman, a master weaver and storyteller, used her web of deceit to trap unsuspecting travelers. And then there was the mischievous Pukwudgie, a small, humanoid creature that played tricks and pranks on humans.

In my investigation, one thing became evident - these tricksters were not mere characters in Native American folklore. They embodied the qualities and characteristics revered by their respective tribes. Their tricky nature served as a reminder of the importance of balance, adaptability, and humility in one's life.

As I delved deeper into their stories, I couldn't help but feel a connection to these mischievous spirits. Their ability to navigate between different realms, manipulate their surroundings, and challenge societal norms resonated with my own journey as a Native American psychic and paranormal investigator.

With every piece of information I gathered, I understood that studying the tricksters wasn't merely about unraveling their mysteries but also understanding myself on a profound level. These spirits were an embodiment of the complexities of the human experience, reminding me that life's trials and tribulations could be overcome through wit, humor, and a touch of mischief.

As I closed my books and reflected on the knowledge I had gained, I couldn't wait to embark on my next adventure - seeking out these beings in the wilds of the Native American lands. Equipped with my psychic abilities, ghost hunting gear, and a deep reverence for the folklore that had shaped me, I was ready to embrace the unpredictable and unruly spirits that roamed these lands.

Little did I know that this journey would challenge me in ways I never could have imagined. The tricksters were waiting, ready to test my abilities, and reveal secrets that would forever alter my perception of the supernatural. And so, with an open mind and a heart filled with both excitement and trepidation, I set off on my quest to uncover the truth behind these mischievous spirits.

Horned Serpents: Enigmatic Beings

As a student of parapsychology, I have always been intrigued by the enigmatic creatures that populate the folklore and mythology of my people. Among these creatures, one stands out in particular - the horned serpent. Its presence in Native American culture is not only steeped in mystery but also carries deep symbolic meaning. In my quest to unravel these mysteries, I embarked on a journey that took me to the heart of ancient legends and spiritual beliefs.

The first step in my exploration was to delve into the origins of the horned serpent. According to Native American lore, these serpents were believed to be supernatural beings that inhabited rivers, lakes, and other bodies of water. They were described as massive, with majestic horns protruding from their heads, and scaly bodies that shimmered in the sunlight. To many tribes, the horned serpent symbolized power, fertility, and protection.

My research led me to various tribes across North America, each with their unique interpretations of the horned serpent. Among the Creek people, for instance, these creatures were known as "Estakwvnayv" and were seen as powerful guardians of the waterways. The Cherokee, on the other hand, believed in the existence of the "Uktena," a horned serpent with magnificent, jewel-encrusted scales. According to legend, the Uktena possessed the ability to bring either good fortune or destruction, depending on how it was approached.

The significance of the horned serpent extended beyond its physical attributes. It represented a connection between the natural and spiritual realms and was often associated with shamanic practices. Many Native American tribes believed that the horned serpent served as a bridge between the physical and spiritual worlds and held the key to unlocking hidden knowledge and wisdom. Shamans would seek visions and guidance from these mystical creatures, hoping to tap into their wisdom and gain insight into the future.

To further deepen my understanding, I turned to the stories and legends passed down through generations. One particularly intriguing tale came from the Ojibwe tribe, where the horned serpent was known as "Misikinubik." According to the story, Misikinubik was a powerful underwater spirit that brought balance and harmony to the world. It was said to embark on a journey every spring to ensure the fertility of the land, and its return was celebrated with rituals and prayers.

Armed with these ancient tales and spiritual insights, I ventured into the realm of symbolism associated with the horned serpent. The horns were often seen as a representation of strength and power, while the serpentine form symbolized transformation and healing. Furthermore, the association between the horned serpent and fertility spoke to the cyclical nature of life, where death and rebirth were interconnected.

Throughout my research, I discovered that the presence of horned serpents in Native American culture extended far beyond mere tales and traditions. Their symbolic significance touched the very core of Native American spirituality, serving as a reminder of our connection to the natural world and the spiritual realm. They represented the delicate balance between life and death, the power of transformation, and the wisdom that can be gained through spiritual journeys.

As I continue my journey as a Native American psychic, ghost hunter, and Bigfoot hunter, the mysteries of the horned serpent remain an ever-present fascination. They are a testament to the rich tapestry of Native American culture and hold within them a vast well of wisdom waiting to be explored and understood.

CHAPTER 3

Scared Rituals

Sweat Lodge: Purification and Renewal

The origins of the sweat lodge can be traced back to ancient times when Native American tribes utilized this ritual as a means of purification and renewal. The sweat lodge was constructed using a framework of willow or other flexible branches, covered with animal hides or blankets. Its circular shape symbolized the cycle of life and the unity of all beings.

Stepping into a sweat lodge, one would immediately notice the intense heat enveloping the small space. The lodge was heated by placing stones, typically volcanic rocks, in a fire outside, and then transferring them inside using specially crafted tongs. These red-hot stones served as a conduit for the spiritual energy that was about to be harnessed.

Once inside the lodge, the participants would enter into a deep state of reflection and prayer. The physical discomfort caused by the extreme heat was a representation of the challenges and hardships that one must endure in order to achieve spiritual purification. As sweat began to pour from their bodies, it symbolized the release of impurities and negative energies.

The ceremonial leader, known as the fire keeper or lodge leader, guided the participants through the ceremony. They would pour water onto the hot stones, creating steam that filled the lodge. This steam, known as "grandfather's breath," represented the presence of the divine and the connection to the spirit world. It was believed that this powerful spiritual energy would cleanse and rejuvenate the participants, both mentally and physically.

The sweat lodge was a space where the veil between the physical world and the spirit world became thin. It provided a sacred space for individuals to connect with their ancestors, spirit guides, and the natural forces of the universe. It was a place for seeking guidance, healing, and spiritual growth.

Throughout history, the sweat lodge has played a crucial role in the Native American communities. It has been used to seek answers, make important decisions, and gather strength for the challenges that lie ahead. It is a practice that continues to be carried on today, not only by Native American tribes but also by individuals from all walks of life who seek a deeper connection with the divine.

As a paranormal enthusiast and spiritual seeker, I have had the privilege of attending various sweat lodge ceremonies throughout my journey. Each experience has been unique and profound. The heat, the steam, and the powerful energy within the lodge have opened doors to new realms of understanding, healing, and spiritual awakening.

The sweat lodge is a testament to the rich spiritual heritage of Native American traditions. It is a reminder of the resilience, wisdom, and spiritual depth of the indigenous people who have inhabited this land for countless generations. By delving into the sacred practice of sweat lodge ceremonies, we can access a profound source of purification and renewal, unlocking the hidden depths of our own spiritual potential.

Smudging: Cleansing the Spirit

My spiritual journey has taken me on a quest to understand the mysteries that lie beyond the physical realm. In my exploration of the supernatural, I have come across various tools and rituals that have played a significant role in Native American traditions. Amongst these, smudging ceremonies have stood out as a powerful means of purifying the spirit.

The practice of smudging can be traced back to ancient times, where indigenous tribes across the Americas partook in this ritual to cleanse their bodies, minds, and spirits. Centuries of wisdom have been passed down through generations, ensuring that the sacred art of smudging continues to thrive in Native American communities to this day.

The concept of smudging revolves around using the smoke of sacred herbs, such as sage, cedar, or sweetgrass, to cleanse and purify oneself or a specific space. These herbs are meticulously gathered, dried, and bundled, with each herb possessing its unique spiritual properties. For example, sage is believed to ward off negative energies, while cedar is said to create a protective barrier against malevolent spirits. Sweetgrass, on the other hand, is considered to invite positive energies and harmonize the environment. The selection of herbs for a smudging ceremony is a highly personal and intuitive process, guided by the individual's intentions and the energy they seek to cultivate.

To conduct a smudging ceremony, the lit herb bundle, known as a smudge stick, is gently waved through the air, allowing the fragrant smoke to disperse and cleanse the space or person. Every nook and cranny, every crevice of the body, is carefully attended to, as the smoke serves as a powerful conductor of the divine energy needed for purification. The act of smudging is not merely physical but deeply rooted in the spiritual understanding that one's inner self requires constant care and purification.

The effects of a smudging ceremony are profound, both on a personal and collective level. On a personal level, smudging can help restore balance and clarity, ridding the body and mind of stagnant energies that impede growth and spiritual development. It awakens one's senses, enhancing intuition and allowing a deeper connection to the spiritual realm. As the smoke rises and dissipates, it carries away negative energies, leaving behind a sense of lightness and renewal.

Furthermore, smudging ceremonies have played a crucial role in Native American communities, serving as collective acts of purification and healing. These ceremonies are often held during important life events, such as births, weddings, or the passing of loved ones. By coming together as a community to smudge, the members pave the way for unity, harmony, and spiritual growth. Such ceremonies allow for the release of negative energies that may have accumulated within the tribe, fostering a renewed sense of connection and healing.

Through my own experiences and countless encounters with spirits, I have come to recognize the profound impact of smudging ceremonies. They offer a gateway to the spiritual realm, providing a space for cleansing, healing, and connection. As I continue to delve into the mysteries of the supernatural, the power of smudging remains an integral part of my journey—a timeless tradition that continues to guide me towards understanding the intricate tapestry of the native paranormal.

Sun Dance: Honoring the Great Spirit

The Sun Dance is a time-honored tradition that has been passed down through generations. It is a sacred ceremony, held during the summer months when the sun is at its zenith, symbolizing the height of spiritual power. As I delved into the history of this ancient ritual, I became captivated by its profound significance.

According to my research, the origins of the Sun Dance date back centuries, to a time when Native American tribes lived in harmony with nature and held a deep reverence for the Great Spirit. The ceremony was seen as a way to honor the divine and seek guidance from the spiritual realm. Through fasting, prayer, and the endurance of physical hardships, participants hoped to gain spiritual insight and demonstrate their devotion to the Great Spirit.

The Sun Dance was not merely a physical ordeal; it was a profound spiritual journey. Participants would prepare themselves mentally, emotionally, and physically weeks in advance. They would purify their bodies and minds through fasting and prayer, seeking spiritual cleansing and clarity.

During the ceremony itself, a large structure, known as the Sun Dance lodge, would be erected in a central location within the tribe's encampment. This sacred space symbolized the connection between the earthly and spiritual realms. The lodge was constructed with great care, using natural materials such as buffalo hides and wooden poles, imbuing it with the essence of the earth.

As the first rays of the sun pierced the dawn, the participants would gather around the lodge, their bodies adorned with ceremonial attire and sacred symbols. The ceremonial leader, known as the Sun Dance chief, would open the proceedings by invoking the presence of the Great Spirit and leading the tribe in prayer and song.

The heart of the ceremony revolved around the Sun Dance pole, which stood tall and proud at the center of the lodge. Adorned with colorful ribbons and symbolic ornaments, the pole represented the axis mundi, the sacred connection between the heavens and earth. Participants would dance and pray around the pole, their movements mirroring the cosmic rhythms and seeking unity with the Great Spirit.

Throughout the ceremony, I could feel the power and energy of the Sun Dance pulsating through the tribe. The rhythm of the drums, the songs of the shamans, and the fervent prayers created an ethereal atmosphere, evoking a profound spiritual awakening. It was a moment where the physical world merged with the spiritual realm, where the veil between the two seemed to vanish.

Through my research and exploration of the Sun Dance ceremony, I gained a deeper appreciation for the Native American spirituality and their connection to the Great Spirit. It became evident to me that the Sun Dance was not merely a cultural tradition; it was a profound expression of faith and reverence for the divine.

As I continue my journey, I carry with me the knowledge and experiences gained from my exploration of the Sun Dance. It has fueled my curiosity and deepened my understanding of the mysteries that lie beyond the veil of our physical existence. The Sun Dance ceremony and its connection to Native American spirituality will forever hold a special place in my heart, reminding me of the sacred and eternal bond between humanity and the Great Spirit. In the 1970 movie A Man Called Horse shows the Vow To The Sun ritual. It was outlawed in 1904 some tribes performed the ritual in secret until .it was believed to be politically dangerous, with the potential of encouraging native to rebel against the reservation system, not to mention cutting of flesh with sharp skewers and fasting for long periods of time. The American Indian religious freedom act in 1978, restoring the right to perform cultural and religious practices.

CHAPTER 4

Supernatural Encounters

Ghostly Apparitions: Spirits From the Other Side

In the depths of time, our ancestors lived in harmony with the spirit world, embracing the belief that the veil separating the two realms was thin. It was a mutual respect, a delicate dance between the corporeal and ethereal beings. However, as the years passed and the modern world encroached upon our sacred lands, this harmony became disrupted.

One of my most haunting encounters took place on the outskirts of a remote native reservation. The whispers of the elders led me deep into the dense woods, where a dilapidated and abandoned house stood as a solemn reminder of forgotten memories. It was said that the spirit of a young girl, taken too soon by illness, dwelled within its decaying walls.

As I entered the house, an icy breeze sent shivers down my spine, making me acutely aware of the presence surrounding me. The air grew thick with a sense of melancholy, and as I ventured further inside, the energy intensified. Shadows danced on the walls, their ethereal forms whispering secrets of the past.

Suddenly, a chill raced through the room, causing goosebumps to rise on my flesh. From the corner of my eye, I caught a glimpse of a figure standing in the doorway, its presence emitting both sadness and longing. It was the ghostly apparition of the young girl, her translucent form flickered before me.

Her eyes, filled with sorrow and longing, pleaded for me to understand her existence. As a psychic, I could hear the echoes of her voice, a soft whisper in the wind recounting the pain and suffering she endured during her short life. It was as if she was trapped in a perpetual cycle of reliving her tragic end.

In that moment, I couldn't help but feel a deep empathy for the young girl's plight. It was a stark reminder that these apparitions were not mere entertainment or imagination, but genuine souls clinging to our world. Their presence, many times misunderstood or dismissed as mere folklore, held a deeper truth about the interconnectedness of life and death.

Throughout my journey as a native paranormal investigator, I have come to appreciate the importance of preserving the stories and experiences of these ghostly apparitions. Their presence within the Native American communities serves as a testament to our connection with the spirit world and the significance of honoring the past.

By bearing witness to these chilling encounters with ghostly apparitions in native American communities, I hope to shed light on the ethereal beings lingering among us, sharing their stories and the history they yearn to convey. Through this understanding, we can bridge the gap between the living and the dead, fostering a sense of reverence for those who have departed from this world but continue to impact our lives from beyond the veil.

In the face of skepticism and dismissal, my mission as a native paranormal investigator remains unwavering. With each encounter, I am reminded of my responsibility to delve deeper into the mysteries of the spirit world, uncovering the hidden truths and bringing them to light. Ghostly apparitions may be elusive, but their presence bears witness to the rich tapestry of Native American communities and the timeless connection we share with the spirits from the other side.

Eerie Lights: The Mystery of Will-o'-the-Wisps

To unravel the enigma of Will-o'-the-Wisps, I delved deep into the annals of native American history, searching for clues and stories that could shed light on this age-old phenomenon. My research led me to a wealth of intriguing tales, passed down through generations, each one imbued with the ethereal glow of these elusive beings.

According to the ancient legends, Will-o'-the-Wisps were believed to be the spirits of lost souls, forever bound to wander the earth. These spirits, it was said, would manifest themselves as floating orbs of light, luring unsuspecting travelers off their intended path. The purpose of these mischievous wanderers remains a subject of debate among scholars and tribes alike. Some believe that their intention is merely to play tricks on weary travelers, leading them astray and leaving them lost in the wilderness. Others, however, hold a more ominous belief, stating that these ethereal lights are malevolent beings who aim to lure their victims to their doom.

One particularly fascinating story dates back to the times of the Cherokee tribe. According to their folklore, Will-o'-the-Wisps were the spirits of mischievous fireflies, seeking to lead humans astray for their own amusement. These glowing insects were said to possess the power to assume human form, their luminous aura disguising their true nature. The Cherokee people believed that one could avoid falling victim to these deceptive lights by wearing a beaded necklace blessed by the tribe's medicine man. This sacred talisman was purported to repel the Will-o'-the-Wisps, keeping them at bay and ensuring safe passage through the darkest of nights.

Further research into native American mythology uncovered similar beliefs among other tribes, each with their own unique perspective on these mysterious lights. The Navajo people, for example, believed that Will-o'-the-Wisps were the souls of witches, condemned to roam the earth and seek out unsuspecting souls to join them in their eternal journey. To the Lakota tribe, these glowing orbs were the embodiment of nature spirits, appearing only to those deemed worthy of witnessing their ethereal presence.

As I pieced together these ancient stories, a pattern began to emerge. The legends of the Will-o'-the-Wisps, while captivating, shared a common thread of caution and vigilance. It became clear that these mysterious lights were not to be taken lightly, and that encountering them required a deep understanding of the natural world and the spiritual realm.

Armed with this newfound knowledge, I embarked on a quest to witness the Will-o'-the-Wisps firsthand. Armed with my psychic abilities and an unwavering determination, I ventured into the dense forests and desolate marshlands said to be their favorite haunts. I set out with a respect for the power and mystery of these otherworldly beings, mindful of the warnings of the ancient tribes.

As I delved deeper into the heart of the wilderness, the air grew heavy with anticipation. My senses heightened, attuned to any anomaly that might indicate the presence of the elusive lights. I scanned the landscape, my eyes straining to catch a glimpse of the ethereal glow that had captivated humankind for centuries.

Hours turned into days, yet the Will-o'-the-Wisps remained elusive. It was as if they were aware of my presence, taunting me with their absence. But I remained undeterred, knowing that my search was far from over.

For now, the enigma of the Will-o'-the-Wisps remains unsolved, their secrets hidden deep within the ancient stories and oral legends of native American tribes. But I am determined to unravel their mysteries, to shed light on their purpose, and to bring their ethereal presence into the realm of understanding.

My journey as a native American psychic, ghost hunter, bigfoot hunter, and UFO enthusiast has brought me face to face with the supernatural. But nothing has prepared me for the enigma of the Will-o'-the-Wisps, those elusive lights that continue to baffle and bewitch the world. And so, with renewed determination, I push forward, ready to uncover the truth behind these enchanting apparitions, one step closer to unraveling the paranormal tapestry of the native American tribes.

Mysterious Cryptids: Legends of Bigfoot and the Wendigo

Exploring the legends surrounding these cryptids has been a personal journey for me, as I delve deep into the rich tapestry of Native American lore. The legends of Bigfoot, also known as Sasquatch, have spanned generations. Natives' tribes across North America have described encounters with this enigmatic creature, believed to inhabit the dense forests and remote wilderness areas. Their accounts speak of a towering, ape-like being, covered in thick hair, with a strong, muscled physique. Some even claim that these creatures possess psychic abilities, allowing them to tap into the spiritual realm.

In my research, I have come across countless stories from various tribes, each with their own unique beliefs and encounters with Bigfoot. The Salish people, for instance, have long revered the creature as a protector of the forests, while the Lakota tribe considers it a sacred being, possessing extraordinary wisdom and knowledge of herbal medicine. These diverse perspectives highlight the deep connection between Native Americans and the natural world, a relationship founded on reverence and harmony.

On the other hand, the legends of the Wendigo paint a starkly different picture. This malevolent creature, often depicted as a cannibalistic entity, has been shrouded in fear and dread. The Wendigo is said to possess an insatiable hunger for human flesh, transforming anyone who resorts to cannibalism into a Wendigo themselves. Many tribes view the Wendigo as a cautionary tale, a harbinger of dark times and the consequences of straying from one's spiritual path.

Throughout my investigations, I have encountered numerous accounts of Wendigo sightings and encounters. Tales of a tall, emaciated figure, with elongated limbs and glowing, red eyes haunt the nightmares of those who dare to venture into the desolate landscapes where the Wendigo is said to roam. The Algonquin people, in particular, have extensively recorded encounters with this creature, passing down stories of brave warriors who have faced and narrowly escaped the clutches of the Wendigo.

While Bigfoot and the Wendigo differ greatly in nature and disposition, their place within Native American culture cannot be denied. Both embody the connection between humans and the natural world, serving as reminders of the power and mystery that exists beyond our understanding. Through the legends and sightings of these cryptids, we are encouraged to seek balance and harmony with the spirits and creatures that occupy the hidden corners of our world.

In my quest to unravel the truth behind these legends, I have ventured deep into the wilderness, investigated numerous reports, and consulted with Native American elders who hold the ancient knowledge of these cryptids. The stories they have shared, the wisdom they have imparted, have guided me on a path that goes beyond mere curiosity. It is a journey that honors the heritage of my people and sheds light on the unexplained phenomena that continue to captivate the hearts and minds of enthusiasts and skeptics alike.

So, as I continue my exploration into the mysterious cryptids that inhabit the realm of the Native American paranormal, I am reminded of the importance of preserving our heritage, honoring the stories passed down through generations, and embracing the mysteries that bind us to the natural world. The legends of Bigfoot and the Wendigo serve as a testament to the enduring power of belief, urging us to look beyond the veil of the ordinary and embrace the extraordinary that lies hidden in the shadows.

Alien Abductions: Native American Close Encounters

The first step in my exploration was to gather and analyze various research conducted on this phenomenon. I scoured through countless reports and interviewed numerous individuals who had experienced these close encounters. The similarities in their descriptions were striking - the bright lights, the sensation of levitation, the lost time, all recurring motifs in their haunting tales.

One particular study that caught my attention focused on the accounts of the Lakota Sioux Tribe in South Dakota. Their oral traditions, passed down through generations, spoke of beings from the stars who visited their ancestors, imparting wisdom and teachings that guided their way of life. But as I delved deeper, I discovered another facet to these encounters - abductions.

According to the research, these abductions were not recent occurrences but had been happening for centuries. They were woven into the very fabric of the Native American cultures, sometimes celebrated as spiritual awakenings, and sometimes feared as malevolent encounters.

One tale that stood out involved a young Lakota woman named Wicincala. She had been taken from her family's encampment while she was gathering firewood near a sacred burial site. Wicincala described being lifted into a blinding beam of light, surrounded by strange creatures with elongated limbs and almond-shaped eyes.

During her abduction, Wicincala underwent a series of experiments. She recalled being examined, prodded, and infused with knowledge that extended far beyond the realm of human understanding. The beings communicated with her telepathically, sharing secrets of the universe, and revealing hidden truths about her people's ancestral connections to the stars.

When Wicincala returned to her tribe, she was met with a mixture of awe and fear. Some regarded her as a chosen one, blessed with extraordinary insights, while others shunned her as tainted by the touch of otherworldly beings. Despite the skepticism she faced, Wicincala embraced her newfound understanding of the universe, becoming a bridge between her people and the extraterrestrial realms.

As I continued my research, I uncovered more and more accounts of Native Americans who had been abducted by aliens. The stories ranged from spiritual encounters with benevolent beings to nightmarish ordeals at the hands of malevolent entities. But what struck me the most was the deeply rooted connection these Native Americans had with the stars.

Their stories resonated with the ancient prophecies passed down in their cultures. Prophecies of cosmic interaction, of a time when humanity would unite with otherworldly forces to usher in a new era of enlightenment. Could it be that these abductions were part of a grand plan, a cosmic awakening for Native Americans?

These revelations sparked a fire within me, pushing me to uncover the truth behind these encounters. I realized that I had a unique opportunity to shed light on this little-explored aspect of Native American paranormal experiences. With each account I uncover, I hope to piece together a puzzle that will not only deepen our understanding of alien abductions but also illuminate the profound connection between Native Americans and the extraterrestrial realm.

As I set out on this investigative journey, armed with my psychic abilities and thirst for knowledge, I hope to uncover the hidden truths that lie within the accounts of these Native Americans who have experienced close encounters. I stand on the precipice, ready to dive into the depths of their stories, to unravel the mysteries of the stars and the intertwining of humanity and the extraterrestrial.

Spiritual Visions: Messages From the Divine

One such story that has left an indelible mark on my soul involves a young Native American boy named Little Elk. Little Elk lived in a small tribe nestled deep within the forested hills of the Appalachian Mountains. From a very young age, he displayed exceptional spiritual abilities, often speaking of visions and messages he received from the divine.

At first, the elders of the tribe were skeptical of Little Elk's claims, dismissing them as the fantasies of an imaginative child. However, as time went on and Little Elk's visions became increasingly accurate and profound, the tribe began to regard him as a vessel through which divine wisdom flowed.

A particularly awe-inspiring vision occurred during the tribe's annual harvest festival. As the dancers swirled around the bonfire, their voices blending with the rhythmic beat of the drums, Little Elk suddenly froze in his tracks. His eyes widened, and it was as if the very essence of the ancestors streamed through his being.

The entire village fell silent in anticipation, their eyes fixed on the young boy. In a hushed voice, Little Elk began to describe a vision he had received. He spoke of a great drought that would ravage their lands, withering their crops and causing immense suffering. But within this bleak prophecy, he also revealed a message of hope, a solution to overcome the impending disaster.

Little Elk proclaimed that the spirit of the rainmaker had appeared to him and imparted a sacred ceremony, one that could summon rain and restore fertility to their lands. The ceremony involved a gathering of the tribe in the sacred grove, where they would chant ancient incantations and dance in unison, their collective energy blending with the natural forces of the universe.

Inspired by Little Elk's vision and deeply rooted in their belief in the interconnectedness of all beings, the tribe wholeheartedly embraced the ceremony. They performed the rain dance with unwavering faith, their voices raised in harmonious chants, their bodies moving in synchrony with the rhythms of the earth.

Days turned into weeks, and weeks turned into months, with no sign of rain. Doubt began to creep into the hearts of some, but their commitment to the sacred ceremony remained unshaken. And then, at the height of their collective despair, as the sun beat relentlessly down upon the parched earth, a single raindrop fell. It was but a whisper from the heavens, a promise of the much-needed nourishment to come.

In that moment, the skies opened up, and a torrential downpour drenched the land. The village rejoiced, their spirits lifted, and they knew that Little Elk's vision had not been in vain. The rainmaker had heard their prayers and delivered them from the drought that threatened their existence.

This story of Little Elk and the rain ceremony is just one of many awe-inspiring tales that Native Americans have passed down through generations. It speaks to the deep spiritual connection our ancestors had with the higher realms and the potency of their messages. These visions not only guided our tribes in the face of adversity but also provided insights into the nature of existence, the delicate balance between the physical and the spiritual, and the interplay of forces that shape our world.

As a native paranormal enthusiast, I am honored to share these stories with you. They serve as a powerful reminder that the spiritual realm is not bound by time or space, and that messages from the divine can be received by anyone who is open to them. May these tales ignite your curiosity, awaken your inner wisdom, and inspire you to delve deeper into the mystical world that exists alongside our own.

CHAPTER 5

Healing Practices

Herbal Medicine: Nature's Remedies

The use of herbs as medicine has been an integral part of Native American culture for centuries. Our ancestors understood the healing properties found in the plants that surrounded them, and they passed down this invaluable knowledge from generation to generation. The wisdom and techniques employed in native American herbal medicine are deeply rooted in our connection to the earth and all its living beings.

Exploring the depths of this ancient practice, I delved into the historical timeline of native American herbal medicine. The timeline revealed a rich tapestry of herbal remedies that have been used to treat various ailments throughout history. From the Native American tribes of the Great Plains using echinacea to boost the immune system, to the Cherokee tribe's use of ginseng for its energy-enhancing properties, each herb has its own unique healing attributes.

I discovered that native American herbal medicine goes beyond the traditional concept of treating physical ailments. It encompasses a holistic approach to healing, considering the spiritual, emotional, and mental well-being of an individual. Native American healers believe that disease and illness are manifestations of imbalances within a person, and herbs can assist in restoring harmony and equilibrium.

The spiritual connection between native American herbal medicine and the natural world cannot be understated. Each herb is believed to possess its own spirit, and its usage involves honoring and communing with these spirits. Native American healers perform rituals and ceremonies to align themselves with the energies of the plants, seeking guidance and wisdom from the spirits that reside within.

The healing journey with native American herbal medicine is deeply personal and transformative. It requires not only a keen understanding of the herbs themselves but also a respect for the delicate balance of nature. By embracing the healing powers of these natural remedies, we reconnect with Mother Earth and remind ourselves of the profound interdependence we share with all living things.

Through my research and personal experiences, I have witnessed the remarkable healing abilities of native American herbal medicine. From soothing salves made of calendula and chamomile to alleviate skin irritations, to drinking sage tea for spiritual purification, the natural remedies have proven to be effective in maintaining and restoring health.

As I continue my exploration of the paranormal and unexplained, I find solace in knowing that native American herbal medicine is a gift from our ancestors that continues to provide healing and solace in the modern world. It is a reminder of the wisdom and interconnectedness that is deeply embedded within our cultural heritage. With every healing plant I encounter, I am reminded of the profound healing powers of nature and the spiritual journey that lies beyond the veil of the physical realm. The herbal remedies of native American medicine truly embody the sacred bond between the human and the natural world. Next time you are in nature, pick out a flower or plant and sit quietly with it, you might discover its secret of healing.

Energy Healing: Balancing the Spirit

The Native American culture has long recognized the concept of energy as the fundamental force that permeates the universe. We understand that everything is connected, and that we are all part of a greater energy web. In this web, balance is crucial. Just like the balance of an ecosystem, our bodies, minds, and spirits also require a state of equilibrium to function at their optimal level.

To achieve this balance, Native American energy healing utilizes various techniques, each rooted in the belief that the body is not merely a physical entity, but also a vessel for spiritual energy. By understanding and manipulating this energy, we can restore harmony and promote overall well-being. One widely practiced method is the use of crystals and stones, believed to possess unique vibrational frequencies that can restore and harmonize the energy within us. Different crystals are associated with specific properties and are used in accordance with the individual's needs.

Another powerful tool in energy healing is the practice of smudging. This involves the burning of sacred herbs, such as sage or sweetgrass, to purify the energy fields and remove any negative or stagnant energy that may be obstructing balance. The smoke acts as a conduit, carrying away unwanted energy and allowing room for positive energy to flow freely.

Aside from these external techniques, Native American energy healing also focuses on internal healing through meditation and connection with nature. Through deep meditation, we can tap into our inner selves, becoming aware of any imbalances and working to heal them. Nature, being a source of pure and harmonious energy, serves as a guide and inspiration on this spiritual journey. By immersing ourselves in the natural world, we can absorb its healing energy and reconnect with the core essence of our being.

The impact of energy healing on the mind, body, and spirit is profound. It surpasses the boundaries of conventional medicine and delves into the energetic realm, where true healing begins. By addressing the root cause of imbalances, energy healing enables the body to restore its natural state of health and vitality. While Western medicine focuses on treating symptoms and ailments, Native American energy healing aims to harmonize the entire being, working on a deep level that goes beyond the physical.

Through my own practice and exploration, I have witnessed remarkable transformations in individuals who have embraced energy healing. The restoration of their spirit, the healing of their bodies, and the clearing of their minds leaves no doubt as to the power and efficacy of this ancient practice. It is my mission to continue delving into these practices, unraveling the mysteries of the universe, and assisting others in their journey towards spiritual balance and well-being.

As a Native American psychic, ghost hunter, Bigfoot hunter, and UFO enthusiast, I am privileged to have a unique perspective on the world and the supernatural. Through my experiences with energy healing, I have come to understand that the unseen forces that surround us are not to be feared but to be embraced and respected. They hold the key to unlocking the deepest mysteries of our existence. And it is through this understanding that we can begin to heal, flourish, and embark on a path to spiritual enlightenment.

Ceremonial Dance: Sacred Movement

There is a sacredness in movement, a profound connection between body and spirit that has been cherished and celebrated by my ancestors for centuries. As a Native American psychic, ghost hunter, bigfoot hunter, and enthusiast of all things paranormal, I have always been drawn to the mystical rituals and ancient traditions that emanate from my rich heritage. Throughout my life, I have delved deep into the realms of the supernatural, unearthing profound truths and secret knowledge that lie hidden beneath the surface of our mundane reality. Amongst these revelations, the therapeutic benefits of ceremonial dances in Native American healing traditions have remained a constantly evolving source of wonder and enlightenment.

To truly grasp the significance of ceremonial dances within Native American healing, it is essential to understand the historical context from which they emerged. For countless generations, my people have sought to commune with the spirits of nature, seeking guidance, healing, and harmony. These dances were not mere performances or entertainment but were sacred movements that carried spiritual significance, connecting the individual to the collective consciousness of the tribe, the spirit world, and the natural world.

The precise origins of these ceremonial dances are shrouded in the mists of time, intertwined with the intricate tapestry of our oral traditions and legends. However, various anthropological researches have shed light on their importance and effectiveness as healing modalities. Early explorers and settlers observed these dances and documented their experiences, providing us with valuable insights into their therapeutic benefits.

One of the most remarkable aspects of ceremonial dances is the profound sense of community they foster. Within Native American tribes, dances served as a unifying force, bringing together individuals from all walks of life, regardless of age, gender, or social status. These dances acted as a conduit for healing through the collective energy generated by the participants. As we moved in rhythmic unison, we became not only connected to one another but also connected to the greater spiritual energies that surrounded us.

Moreover, ceremonial dances were believed to possess the power to heal both physical and spiritual ailments. During these dances, the body became a vessel through which the divine energies flowed, cleansing, and restoring balance to the individual. Every step, every sway, and every beat of the drum resonated with the beating heart of Mother Earth, imbuing us with her healing power. As I danced, I could feel the energy coursing through my veins, as if I was both a conduit and recipient of its transformative force.

But to truly experience the therapeutic benefits of ceremonial dances, one must understand that it is not a mere physical act but a deeply spiritual journey. It requires an open heart, a receptive mind, and a willingness to let go of the burdens that weigh us down. When I first embarked on this path, I had to shed my preconceived notions and surrender myself to the ancient wisdom that guided every step of the dance. In doing so, I discovered a profound sense of liberation, an unburdening of the soul that allowed for deep healing to take place.

Looking back on my journey as a native paranormal investigator, I can confidently say that the therapeutic benefits of ceremonial dances in Native American healing traditions are a testament to the profound wisdom and interconnectedness of our ancestors. These dances are not simply relics of the past but living embodiments of a truth that transcends time and space. They are an invitation to step into the sacred circle of life, to embrace the healing power of movement, and to experience the profound connections that unite us all.

As I continue my exploration into the paranormal mysteries of the world, I carry with me the sacred knowledge gained from these ceremonial dances. They have become an integral part of my own healing journey, guiding me towards a greater understanding of myself and the world around me. Through each step of the dance, I honor the spirits of my ancestors, tapping into their wisdom, and forging a path towards healing for myself and the countless souls I encounter along the way.

Sound Healing: Vibrations of Harmony

In order to fully explore the depths of sound healing techniques used by native Americans, I embarked on a journey that took me back in time. I delved into the rich history of my ancestors and uncovered a profound connection between sound and healing. It became apparent that sound has always played a significant role in native American cultures, with various tribes utilizing different methods to achieve balance and restoration.

One of the earliest documented forms of sound healing among native Americans is through the use of drums. The rhythmic beats produced by these sacred instruments reverberate through the air, penetrating deep into the soul. The vibrations created by the drums have the power to restore harmony within oneself and with the natural world. I witnessed this first-hand during a sacred drumming ceremony with a tribe elder, where the entrancing rhythms transported us to a place of inner peace and tranquility.

Another fascinating aspect of native American sound healing lies in the use of vocalization and chanting. Different tribes have their own unique chants, each possessing its own specific purpose. These chants are believed to invoke spiritual energies and facilitate healing on a deeper level. I had the privilege of attending a healing ceremony led by a native American medicine woman, and the experience was beyond words. The resonance of her voice, combined with the ancient chants, created a captivating symphony that seemed to reverberate through every cell in my body. I felt a profound shift in my energy and a sense of inner harmony that lingered long after the ceremony ended.

Flutes are yet another tool employed by native American healers to promote spiritual and physical well-being. The haunting melodies produced by these instruments have the power to soothe the mind and awaken deep emotions. During a journey to a tribal reservation, I had the honor of witnessing a flute player perform a healing melody. The enchanting music seemed to transcend the physical realm, transporting us to a realm of pure serenity. I closed my eyes and allowed the ethereal notes to wash over me, feeling a sense of balance and rejuvenation coursing through my entire being.

Exploring the transformative effects of sound healing techniques used by native Americans has not only deepened my understanding of ancient traditions but has also provided me with a renewed appreciation for the power of sound. The vibrations that emerge from these practices have the ability to awaken dormant energies within us, harmonizing the body, mind, and spirit. It is a testament to the profound wisdom of native American cultures and serves as a reminder that the path to well-being can often be found in the most unexpected places.

Soul Retrieval: Healing the Past

Paranormal enthusiast, my journey has led me down many fascinating paths. From hunting ghosts to chasing Bigfoot, and even seeking out UFO encounters, my thirst for the supernatural has never ceased. However, there is one area of my research that holds a special place in my heart and has provided me with profound insights into the human psyche - soul retrieval. This ancient practice, deeply rooted in indigenous cultures, has the power to restore wholeness and heal the wounds of our past.

The concept of soul retrieval dates back centuries, spanning across various civilizations and cultures. While the specifics may differ, the underlying principle remains the same - a part of our essence, our soul, can become fragmented or lost due to traumatic experiences. In these instances, we may feel incomplete, disconnected, or stuck in a cycle of emotional pain.

Our ancestors recognized the importance of the soul and its role in our spiritual and emotional well-being. They understood that by addressing the wounds of the past, we could find healing and regain our sense of self. Through ceremonies, rituals, and the guidance of wise elders, they developed the practice of soul retrieval.

The process of soul retrieval involves journeying into the depths of one's psyche to reclaim the fragments of the soul that have been scattered throughout time. It requires a connection with the spirit world, an unwavering belief in the unseen, and a willingness to confront our deepest fears and traumas. Although it can be a challenging and emotional undertaking, the rewards are immeasurable.

During my own exploration of soul retrieval, I have delved into ancient texts, consulted with shamans, and undertaken numerous journeys into the realm of the unconscious. Through these experiences, I have witnessed the profound impact that soul retrieval can have on individuals who have suffered from past traumas.

The process of soul retrieval often begins with identifying the traumatic event or series of events that caused the soul to fragment. Through deep meditation, regression therapy, and guidance from spiritual mentors, we can trace our emotional wounds back to their origin. This, in itself, is a cathartic and transformative journey, as it allows us to confront our pain and confront the source of our internal strife.

Once the event or events have been identified, the shaman or spiritual guide facilitates the journey to retrieve the lost fragments of the soul. This can be done through various means - meditation, trance-like states, or even physical journeys to sacred sites. The purpose is to reconnect with the parts of ourselves that have been lost or abandoned, bringing them back into our consciousness and embracing them with love and understanding.

The process of soul retrieval is a powerful catalyst for healing. It allows us to acknowledge and validate our past traumas, offering us an opportunity to release the emotional burdens that have weighed us down for so long. By integrating these lost aspects of ourselves, we can move forward with a greater sense of wholeness, self-acceptance, and inner peace.

In my own practice, I have witnessed individuals undergoing profound transformations through soul retrieval. I have seen survivors of abuse reclaim their self-worth, individuals burdened by grief find solace, and those trapped in cycles of self-sabotage break free and embrace their true potential. Soul retrieval offers a path towards healing that is deeply spiritual, deeply personal, and deeply transformative.

As we continue our journey through the realms of the paranormal, it is important to remember the importance of addressing the wounds of our past. Soul retrieval, although ancient in practice, offers a timeless solution to the pain and suffering that has plagued humanity throughout history. By embracing this sacred practice, we can find healing, restoration, and the profound sense of wholeness we all strive for. So let us venture forth, not only into the realms of the unknown, but also into the depths of our own souls, for it is there that true healing lies.

CHAPTER 6

Spiritual wisdom

The Circle of Life: Harmony and Balance

In the vast tapestry of Native American cultures, the concept of the circle of life holds a significant place. It is a philosophy that embraces the interconnectedness of all living beings, where every element of existence is intricately woven together. At its core, the circle of life teaches us that everything is part of a greater whole, and each individual has a crucial role to play in maintaining the delicate balance of the universe.

The teachings of the circle of life emphasize the importance of acknowledging and honoring the interconnectedness of all life forms. Just as the sun and the moon coexist in perfect harmony, so too should every living creature strive to find their own place within the cosmic web of existence. By embracing this interconnectedness, we are reminded of the sacredness of all life, and the responsibilities we bear as custodians of this Earth.

One of the key aspects of living in harmony and balance according to the circle of life philosophy is understanding the role of nature in our lives. Native American cultures hold a deep reverence and respect for the natural world, recognizing that Mother Earth provides everything we need to nourish our bodies, minds, and souls. By harmonizing our actions with the cycles of nature, we learn to coexist harmoniously, nurturing the earth as she nourishes us in return.

The beauty of the circle of life philosophy lies in its holistic approach to understanding existence. It teaches us that just as every individual has a role to play, so do the elements of the natural world. Native Americans are keen observers of nature, recognizing the subtle signs and messages that surround us. From the gentle rustle of the wind to the flight of birds in the skies, nature communicates with us if we are willing to listen. By attuning ourselves to these messages, we can gain a deeper understanding of our place within the circle of life and find guidance in our own journey.

Living in harmony and balance also entails cultivating a strong sense of spirituality. Native American cultures believe in the power of the unseen world, where spirits and energies intertwine with our own reality. Through ancient rituals and practices, they establish a connection with the spiritual realm, seeking guidance and wisdom from ancestors and spirit guides. This spiritual connection acts as a compass, guiding them towards a balanced and harmonious existence.

In my quest as a ghost hunter, Bigfoot hunter, and UFO enthusiast, I find solace and inspiration in the teachings of the circle of life. It serves as a constant reminder that paranormal phenomena are not detached from the fabric of existence but are simply another expression of the interconnectedness of all things. And it is through this understanding that I navigate the realms of the unknown, seeking answers and unraveling the mysteries that constantly intrigue and captivate me.

The native concept of the circle of life and its teachings on harmony and balance are timeless and profound. By embracing these teachings, we can cultivate a deeper sense of connection with the world around us and find our place within the vast tapestry of existence. It is a philosophy that reminds us that we are not just individuals moving through life but integral parts of a greater whole.

In this realization, we can truly live in harmony and balance, nurturing ourselves, our fellow beings, and the earth that sustains us all.

The Medicine Wheel: Spiritual Guidance

The Medicine Wheel is a circular representation of the interconnectedness of all things in the universe. It is a powerful symbol that reflects the cyclical nature of life and offers insight into the spiritual paths that we embark upon. Each direction on the wheel holds its unique energy and significance, providing us with a roadmap for personal transformation.

To fully grasp the depths of the Medicine Wheel's guidance, it is crucial to explore its sacred symbolism and the teachings associated with each direction. The wheel is divided into four cardinal directions, each representing a specific aspect of our being and the world around us.

Starting with the East, we begin our journey with the energy of the rising sun. This direction symbolizes new beginnings, spiritual awakening, and the element of air. The East encourages us to embrace the dawning of each day with a renewed sense of purpose and to open ourselves up to the limitless possibilities that lie ahead. Through meditation and introspection, we can cultivate clarity of mind and connect with our higher selves, allowing us to embark on a path of personal growth and transformation.

Moving clockwise around the wheel, we encounter the South. The South represents the element of fire and the warmth of the midday sun. It is here that we explore our passions, creativity, and personal power. The teachings of the South urge us to embrace our authentic selves, to celebrate our unique gifts and talents, and to ignite the flame of passion within our hearts. By harnessing this energy, we can tap into our creative potential and manifest our deepest desires.

Continuing our journey, the West awaits us. This direction symbolizes the element of water and the setting sun, representing introspection, emotional healing, and transformation. In the West, we confront our fears and shadows, diving deep into the depths of our subconscious. It is through this exploration that we find the keys to our emotional healing, uncover hidden truths, and embrace the transformative power of forgiveness and acceptance. The West reminds us to honor our emotions, allowing them to flow like water, and to trust in the process of change.

Finally, we arrive at the North, the direction of the element of earth and the wisdom of the ancestors. In the North, we connect with the ancient wisdom that has been passed down through generations. Here, we seek guidance and gain insight from our ancestors, spirit guides, and elders. The teachings of the North remind us of the importance of grounding ourselves in the physical world, nurturing our bodies, and honoring the interconnectedness of all living beings.

Within the sacred space of the Medicine Wheel, we find the opportunity for personal growth and spiritual development. It is a place of introspection, where we can find solace, guidance, and healing. By aligning ourselves with the energies of each direction and embracing their teachings, we can navigate the challenges of life with grace and wisdom.

As a Native American psychic and ghost hunter, I have witnessed firsthand the power of the Medicine Wheel in bridging the gap between the physical and spiritual realms. It is through this ancient wisdom that I have been able to navigate the paranormal world, communicate with spirits, and unravel the mysteries of the unknown. The Medicine Wheel has served as my compass, guiding me in my pursuit of understanding the supernatural.

In my quest for knowledge and spiritual enlightenment, I have also found myself drawn to the mysteries of Bigfoot and UFOs. These phenomena, often dismissed or overlooked by mainstream society, hold a profound connection to the indigenous wisdom and the teachings of the Medicine Wheel. It is through the lens of the Medicine Wheel that I have come to understand the significance of these elusive beings and their interactions with humanity.

The Medicine Wheel offers us a pathway to connect with the unseen realms and tap into the ancient wisdom that lies dormant within us all. It reminds us that we are not mere observers in this vast universe but active participants in the unfolding of our spiritual journeys. By delving into the sacred symbolism of the Medicine Wheel and embracing its guidance, we can unlock the hidden potentials within ourselves and forge a deeper connection with the world around us.

As I continue my exploration into the paranormal and delve deeper into the mysteries that surround us, the Medicine Wheel remains my steadfast companion. It is a reminder of the profound interconnectedness of all things and a source of spiritual guidance that transcends time and space. With each step I take on this spiritual path, I am guided by the wisdom of the Medicine Wheel and the eternal teachings it holds.

The Seven Sacred Directions: Connecting with the Divine

In Native American cultures, the concept of the Seven Sacred Directions goes beyond mere cardinal directions. It represents a sacred map that connects us to the spiritual realm and acts as a guide for our journey through life. Each direction holds its own unique energy, symbolism, and teachings from the divine.

To truly understand the spiritual significance of the Seven Sacred Directions, one must immerse themselves in the rich cultural beliefs passed down from generation to generation. For me, this meant delving into ancient texts, speaking to elders, and participating in sacred ceremonies to gain a deeper understanding of the sacredness of these directions.

Starting with the East, I discovered that it represents new beginnings, the rising sun, and the element of air. It symbolizes enlightenment, mental clarity, and the birth of ideas. It is the direction of the mind, where we seek knowledge and wisdom. The East teaches us to embrace change and to allow ourselves to be reborn into a higher spiritual plane.

Moving clockwise, I explored the significance of the South. The South represents the warm breath of the sun, the element of fire, and the realm of emotions. It is associated with passion, creativity, and the nurturing energy of Mother Earth. The South teaches us to listen to our hearts, to follow our instincts, and to cultivate a deep connection with all living beings.

Continuing on, I delved into the spiritual teachings of the West. The West is the direction of the setting sun, the element of water, and the realm of introspection. It represents the twilight hours, where darkness and light merge, and mirrors the cycle of life and death. The West teaches us to embrace our shadow selves, to confront our fears and limitations, and to find balance within the duality of existence.

Next, I explored the profound symbolism of the North. The North is associated with the winter season, the element of earth, and the deep wisdom of our ancestors. It represents introspection, stillness, and the path to spiritual enlightenment. The North teaches us to connect with our ancestral roots, to seek guidance from those who have walked before us, and to honor the earth as a sacred entity.

With the remaining three directions, I discovered the spiritual essence of the Upper World, the Lower World, and the Center. The Upper World represents the realm of heavenly beings, celestial energies, and divine guidance. It is an infinite source of wisdom that connects us to the cosmos and reminds us of our divine nature.

On the other hand, the Lower World represents the realm of spirits, ancestors, and animal guides. It is a place of deep connection with the natural world, where we can learn from the wisdom of animals and seek guidance from our ancestors. The Lower World teaches us to respect and honor all living beings and to understand our interconnectedness with the web of life.

Lastly, the Center symbolizes the sacred space within us all, the place where the energies of the Seven Sacred Directions converge. It is the point of balance, harmony, and healing. The Center teaches us to find our true selves, to listen to our inner voice, and to cultivate a deep connection with the divine within.

Discovering the spiritual significance of the Seven Sacred Directions has been a transformative journey for me. It has allowed me to understand the interconnectedness of all things and to align myself with the divine energies that permeate our existence. Through the teachings of the Seven Sacred Directions, I have learned to embrace the mysteries of the unknown, to seek enlightenment, and to walk the path of spiritual growth and transformation.

The Power of Prayer: Communication with the Spirit World

Growing up on the reservation, prayer was interwoven into the fabric of our daily lives. It was not simply a ritualistic practice but a profound and intimate form of communication with our ancestors and the spirits around us. It was through prayer that we sought guidance, healing, and protection from unseen forces that both fascinated and frightened us.

My first real encounter with the power of prayer occurred when I embarked on a ghost-hunting expedition in an abandoned and dilapidated asylum. The air was thick with a palpable sense of unrest, as if the spirits of the forgotten patients still roamed the desolate hallways. Armed with my psychic abilities and a humble heart, I stood in the center of the asylum's decayed chapel and began to pray.

With each whispered word, the atmosphere shifted, as if the invisible veil that separated the living from the dead was momentarily lifted. Shadows danced in the flickering candlelight, and a whispering wind echoed through the halls. It was in that moment that I realized the true power of prayer. It was not merely a string of words, but a conduit through which our intentions and desires could be carried to the spirit world.

But prayer was not limited to encounters with restless spirits. In my pursuit of understanding the elusive phenomenon of bigfoot and UFOs, prayer became an integral part of my investigations. Before venturing into the dense forests where sightings had occurred, I would sit in sacred silence, offering my prayers to the spirits of the land. I felt a deep connection with the earth beneath my feet and the infinite sky above me, as if my words were being carried by the wind and whispering among the trees.

Through this bond forged by prayer, I began to witness the miraculous. In moments of communion with nature and the universe, signs would manifest, guiding me to the truths hidden within the depths of the wilderness. It was as if the spirit world itself recognized my devotion and chose to reveal its secrets to those who approached it with respect and reverence.

In the spirit world, there is no separation between the physical and the metaphysical, the seen and the unseen. It is a realm of interconnectedness, where prayers are not heard but felt. They resonate within the deepest recesses of our soul, drawing us closer to the wisdom and guidance that lies beyond our mortal realm.

Through my extensive research and personal experiences, I have discovered that prayer is not bound by borders or cultural barriers. It is a universal language that transcends time and space, speaking to the innate longing within us all to connect with something greater than ourselves.

So, I invite you to join me on this extraordinary journey as we explore the transformative power of prayer in Native American spirituality and its role in connecting with the spirit world. Together, we will unravel the mysteries hidden within the depths of our souls and bear witness to the profound and awe-inspiring beauty of the spirit realm.

Free Resources

The following prayers and incantations are available at durindajstewart.com/free-tools/. Simply join for free to receive notifications when I release new tools, resources, and other free stuff. While you're there check out my podcast, Wife of a Demon Hunter, which you can also find on Spotify.

- **Smudging Prayer**
    - Utilized to cleanse the body, aura, and energy of a private or ceremonial area.
- **Releasing Past Life Vows**
    - Releases you from old vows that no longer serve your highest good.
- **Eviction Notice of Evil Spirits**
    - Cleansing prayer to bless a space and evict any evil spirits.
- **Cutting the Cords of Toxic**
    - A prayer for the energy of love serving the highest good of all involved.

Visit **DurindaJStewart.com** for more information.

Made in the USA
Columbia, SC
12 July 2024

7386ace7-5dff-4f5f-a6f4-d7426fa66e99R01